Y0-CAF-122

RETIRED

Good Busy

CHAPEL HILL
PUBLIC LIBRARY

Julia Scatliff O'Grady

GOOD
BUSY

PRODUCTIVITY,
PROCRASTINATION,
AND THE ENDLESS
PURSUIT OF BALANCE

RCWMS | Durham, NC

2012

Good Busy: Productivity, Procrastination,
and the Endless Pursuit of Balance
Copyright © 2012 Julia Scatliff O'Grady

All rights reserved. Printed in the United States of America.
No part of this book may be used or reproduced in any manner
whatsoever without written permission except in the case of brief
quotations embodied in critical articles or reviews. For information, contact RCWMS, 1202 Watts Street, Durham, NC 27701,
919-683-1236, rcwmsnc@aol.com.

Design by Chris Crochetière, BW&A Books, Inc.
Printed in the United States of America

ISBN 978-0-9722035-6-2

Library of Congress Control Number: 2012936036

First Edition, 2012
10 9 8 7 6 5 4 3 2 1

Copies of the book may be ordered from:

RCMWS
1202 Watts Street
Durham, NC 27701
www.rcwms.org
rcwmsnc@aol.com

For Dad, James Howard Scatliff, M.D.

Contents

Acknowledgments

Ten years ago, I announced that I was going to write a book about time. Many thanks to everyone who helped me keep the faith.

First, I offer thanks to my husband Brian, my guardian angel. My daughter Frances is my muse, while my son Trygve has been a witty companion. I love you all.

Thanks to my parents, Irene and Jim Scatliff. They have always modeled a life of hard work and compassion. My sister Amy exemplifies a kindness that is singular. Uncle Harvey, Chris, and Henry, my Minnesota relatives, hold the key to good busy. Since before I knew how to tell time, Margo MacIntyre has been my friend. I am grateful to the O'Grady family, especially Betty and John, who raised such a beautiful son and provide me with constant welcome.

I give thanks to everyone who agreed to be interviewed. Without their words and generosity, there would be no book: Esther, Shawn Amos, Kari Andrade, Alex Byrd, Sandy Dang, Joe Kennedy, Louisa Meacham, Tom Rankin, Tom Spuhler, and Debra Westenskow.

I am grateful to my editor, Jeanette Stokes, who has helped to advance this project with great pluck and insight. *Good Busy* would not be in your hands without her. I am indebted to the hard work of other RCWMS women who read, proofed, and helped bring this book into the world, especially Liz Dowling-Sendor, Pat Green, Margie Hattori, Marcy Lytle, Marya McNeish, and Lori Pistor. Nancy Rosebaugh brought a grace and tenacity to the manuscript toward the end that calmed any remaining fears. Casey and Matt Elia are inspired photographers. Thanks to the A.J. Fletcher Foundation for the travel award that made a trip to Los Angeles, California and Las Vegas, Nevada possible.

Thank you, Union College. You opened your arms wide to my family and me in 2002 so I could begin this journey. You enabled us to join your community for two academic years, even with a one-year-old and a three-year-old in tow. Special thanks go to Wayne Meisel for helping us get to Barbourville, David and Lynne Joyce, Garry Payne, Kelly Eikleberry, Anne and Paul Peterson, Candy Wood, and Julie Iliff. Most of all, I am grateful to Lisa Jordan, who fixed up a cozy home for us, took long walks with me, and whose friendship continues to be like no other.

In 2006, I put down the *Good Busy* manuscript and entered graduate school to pursue a PhD in Communication Studies. I wrote a master's thesis entitled "Life, Liberty, and the Pursuit of Busyness," which was supervised by Dennis Mumby, Pat Parker, Mark Robinson, and mentor, Julia T. Wood. These scholars have helped me further develop my thoughts through the rigors of academic discipline. I thank JTW for perspective the breadth of the equator.

Certain friends became what I call *butt-kickers*. Stu Horwitz was the first to provide professional advice and to say he liked the phrase "Good Busy." Ed Cohen's career change inspired mine. Mark Gerzon was honest enough to tell me I could do better. John Beilenson reminded me not to get too complicated. Donna Campbell and Georgann Eubanks cheered me on. Tony Deifell and Mardie Oakes kept me on point. Sharon Loh helped edit the manuscript. Tim Walter, Kristin Bass, and Caroline Durham provided invaluable support. Chloe Breyer, Faulkner Fox, Rosanne Haggerty, Peggy Payne, Billy Shore, Julien Phillips, and Libby Turner made insightful comments on earlier versions of the manuscript. Claudia Horwitz knows just how to love me through her words and deeds of everyday and interstellar encouragement.

Introduction

Saint Augustine stands under a cloak of stars on the North Africa coast in the fourth century CE. Known for his powers of oration and charisma, he has one gnawing problem: he is flummoxed by his relationship with time. "What is time, God?" he asks as he paces along the shore. "I know what it is if no one asks me what it is; but if I want to explain it to someone who has asked me, I find that I do not know." As he walks and talks, he continues, "My soul is on fire to solve this very complicated enigma." Soon, however, Augustine realizes that God cannot help him. He must learn how to relate to time on his own.

Fast-forward to the late twentieth century CE. Stephen Covey, author of the best-selling *The 7 Habits of Highly Effective People,* stands in front of an audience with the following props: two transparent plastic buckets, a bag of green gravel, and a collection of multi-colored rocks, labeled as Important Client, Exercise, Major Project, Relationship, Family, Church, and Community. Next to Covey is a volunteer from the audience, a businesswoman wearing a red suit and pumps. Her hair is pulled back to reveal professional gold knotted earrings. "Do you ever feel like you're getting bogged down in the thick of thin things?" Covey asks of the woman. As she says yes, Covey picks up the bag of green gravel and nearly fills one of the two plastic buckets with it.

Covey then asks the woman to read aloud the labels written on each rock as she attempts to fit them into the bucket on top of the green gravel. Dutifully, the woman begins the assignment, soon realizing she cannot fit all of the rocks into the bucket. As she moves the gravel, attempting to situate the rocks deeper in the bucket, the camera pans to the audience bursting with the laughter of self-recognition. Covey says to the woman, "You can work out of a different paradigm altogether—you can do anything you want." She starts all over again, putting the big rocks in the bucket first. In this second effort, she fits both the big rocks and the gravel into the bucket with ease.

In my mind, Covey's "big rocks" exercise is somewhere on the other side of the spectrum from Augustine's plea on the beach. Where Augustine struggles to understand what time is—and, implicitly, its meaning for finite creatures—Covey illustrates the dilemma of temporality with buckets, gravel, and big rocks. Time management seminars like the one I describe address people's frustration with the busyness of modern life. In ersatz worlds of peppermints, notepads, pens, water pitchers, planners, and perky trainers, participants vow to practice greater efficiency in their public and private lives. Inside hotel ballrooms across the United States, trainers project an optimistic certainty that time can be managed through deliberate acts of control. Participants are taught to place all of life's concerns and responsibilities into one of four quadrants and to realize that not all urgent matters are important. Time becomes a quantifiable resource to be mastered through better technology, products, goal-setting, and personal organization skills.

I have been a regular in the "time ballroom." At first, I attended these seminars with a desire to fix myself, expecting the trainer to help me build a better relationship with time through the acquisition of skills. I had hopes of being more punctual and organized as I sought to end my entrenched habits of procrastination. But as I returned to my everyday life, I found I did not use their time management systems. The certainty I felt in the ballroom evaporated as unused planners piled up beside my desk. After a while, I came to terms with the reality that having a better relationship with time does not require shortcuts or systems. Instead, it requires a patient practice of trial and error and taking advantage of opportunities for reflection.

For a while, I led time management seminars on my own. I discovered that if participants could think more intentionally about how to bring incremental or organic change to their lives, a system was no longer necessary. The secret to effective use of time appeared to be not so much teaching new time management systems as helping people think creatively about their existing frameworks for getting things done. Intrigued by the breakthroughs I witnessed during these seminars, I began to interview people to discover their relationship with their own busyness. I reasoned that the best practices I witnessed could serve as inspiration for other people's lives and my own. I learned how people I admire dealt with the challenges of managing time by listening to their stories about their everyday lives. As I listened, I honed in on one or two words that each person used to express the challenges and strategies for getting through their days. Each word or phrase became one of the ten lessons about the experience of busyness in this book.

Busyness, for many of us, has come to characterize our relationship with time. Just notice how we respond to the most basic everyday question, "How are you?" with some rendition of "busy" instead of "fine." We count the many ways we are busy instead of reflecting upon our current state of being. If being busy is now the predominant paradigm for our relationship with time, then surely there is a way to experience a good busyness in our everyday lives. Perhaps a more reflective approach to time management can help us develop a more thoughtful relationship with time. In reflective time management, we situate ourselves somewhere between the open-ended query of Saint Augustine and the technical confidence of Stephen Covey. I call this the search for good busy.

So what is good busy? Good busy is not an oxymoron. The phrase represents the experience of the moments in everyday life when our actions come close to matching our intentions for ourselves and for the world around us. While the experience of good busy is not always present in the ebb and flow of everyday life, we can be patient and carry on in its absence, while planning for its return. My point is that good busy, a balance between action and reflection in our everyday lives, is always possible. We get better at it as we go.

This book represents my own search for good busy. The chapter titles—Buffer, Routine, Mirror, Tunnel, Sliver, Geological, Sequence, Gungee, Milk (your cows), and Hunt—represent ten fascinating people I interviewed. Their words and practices helped me deepen my ongoing search for good busy. In each conversation, I asked people to describe their relationship with busyness. Without exception, people could distinguish good from bad busy. Good busy represented some period of time—an hour, a day, a week or more—when life went well. Their days were full and fulfilling. They had a lot to do, and yet they were at peace with their daily motion. By contrast, people spoke of a bad busy that was the opposite—a busyness that was frenetic, exhausting, and not sustainable. Bad busy was motion without thought and was detrimental to individuals and to the world around them. The trick is to reach toward good busy and steer clear of the bad.

I went in search of good busy, not because I wanted to stop being busy, but because I wanted to learn how to make better choices in my own daily life. The practices I learned from the people I write about are now anchors in my life, meant for days that have become disorganized, turbulent, and even chaotic as a result of the many demands and stressors at work, at home, and in my community. While no one I interviewed professed to be a time management expert, and everyone balked at the suggestion, they each have a lesson to share about their own approach to busyness. I know because I am the first adopter of these practices in my own life and in my role as a teacher.

This search for good busy has further educated me on the role that social class, educational level, and earning potential play in shaping the experience of busyness. If you earn the minimum wage or are financially insecure, your ability to experience good busy may be encumbered by economic forces beyond your immediate control. That said, almost all of the people interviewed have faced financial challenges, and their stories incorporate their particular responses. For this reason, I believe each example to be of relevance to most readers.

I am passionate about the topic of time, in part because I see so many people suffering from feelings of guilt and incompetence that arise from our everyday choices. While multitasking and efficiency have their place, they are also threats to our health. My hope is that you will find greater peace as you try out some of the practices suggested in this book. Ultimately, reckoning with time is a personal journey. While the people profiled may serve as inspiration, you must discover practices of your own. What would you say if I interviewed you? What words or stories would describe your journey? Everyone has wisdom and life experience. What will you do?

1 Buffer
Keep a margin.

When Kari Andrade was three years old, she turned on the water in her third floor bathroom and walked downstairs to the kitchen. The next thing she knew, water was cascading down the staircase. Kari's mother screamed when she saw the rushing water. From that day, Kari vowed never to lose control of any other situation. Remarkably, that is pretty much what has happened. The experience of rushing water forever changed how Kari approaches her daily life. In our conversations, the word "buffer" appeared again and again in reference to the little girl, now a grown woman, who never quite got over the experience of cascading water. Buffer is the first practice to consider. Attempt to live with a margin.

As a lifelong practitioner of buffering, Kari builds in extra time at every turn by adding more time than she thinks a task will really require. She predicts the duration of any experience and adds extra time. In so doing, she acknowledges the uncertainty of life, that no one knows exactly how long it will take to get from here to there. The message is to budget more time than we think we need. When I remember to buffer, my days feel much calmer.

Kari is 5'9" with salt-and-pepper shoulder-length curly hair. A voice that loops from the lowest pitch to a soprano transports ready and contagious laughter. In college, she set records in both the shot put and discus. Today she is an avid walker and triathlete. Not a woman of pretense, she dresses up for work, but at home prefers a t-shirt, shorts and no bra.

Kari's parents divorced when she was young; after that, she and her sister lived primarily with their dad. Kari's stepmother, a literary agent, brought stability to Kari's childhood and encouraged a love of books and learning in their home. Her father Eddie—a professor, alderman, restaurateur, and political activist—inspired professionalism and competence. He told me that he thrived on discussions at dinner with his two daughters. "I wanted them to be engaged in the world," he said. "I wanted them to change the world, poor darlings. I was not stern. I was a let-it-happen hippie." Eddie and Kari argued over current events, such as what was best for China. Eddie was a communist, while Kari was an unabashed capitalist from a young age. When Kari was ten, her dad enrolled her in an experimental school. After only a month, she told her dad she wanted to go to a school that would help her get a good job. In high school, Kari trumped her dad by learning to speak Mandarin, so she could live in China, first as a student and later as a businesswoman. While her family "just let life happen," Kari has always been a planner. She carries a pencil and an appointment book everywhere she goes, buys clothes for her eleven-year-old daughter Allison years before she can wear them, and plans the family dinner menu a month in advance. Her vacations are arranged for the next three years.

Kari and I were roommates during our first year of college. By the time I got to the dorm, Kari had made her bed, folded her clothes and put them away, hung posters, and arranged her toiletries. She set up crates filled with sweaters of every hue as a buffer against the cold Minnesota winters. She broke the ice by telling me where she had gotten each sweater and described all of the bargains she had found. Since that first day, Kari and I have been close friends. Nearly twenty years later, when we both had babies and were living in North Carolina, we grew even closer.

I was somewhat self-conscious in my role as interviewer with Kari and nervous about my own punctuality. If I showed up late, I would feel I had failed at buffering and knew better than to blame my tardiness on a traffic jam, a train, or a last-minute phone call. When I was on time, I wondered if Kari secretly took the credit for my success. While I thought I was doing research for a book about busyness, I soon discovered I was a struggling adopter of the practices I was collecting. During our conversations about the buffer, Kari helped me understand the practice through the following formula:

$$H + \tfrac{1}{3}H = T$$

H is the symbol for duration, the amount of time you think you will need to drive across town or finish an assignment. Take one third of H and add it to your original approximation of the time required. T is the sum total that will ensure punctuality or early completion of a task.

How do you master the buffer? Kari says to begin with daily observation. She took note of how long it took to get to the store, to work, or to her daughter's school. She clocked the actual time it took to buy groceries, get to a meeting across town, or call a friend. She committed these times to memory. With careful observation, she accounted for the true volume of her daily responsibilities.

"When you don't know the duration of an experience, you ask or do a little research," Kari said. So many people ignore this basic measure. They head off on a journey without critical information that some person or some website could have told them. Learning how to buffer means setting aside time for road construction and possible detours. If what you plan to do is really important, put in more buffer. Hard as it is to think about, as Kari says, "something really bad might happen."

Kari's concept of the buffer may have begun with her childhood experience of the rushing water, but she refined the practice as an adult in Amsterdam and Beijing. Instead of blaming tardiness on cultural differences or unreliable assistance, Kari buffered situations to determine how best to proceed and be on time. For example, when she worked as a business executive for Cargill in China, she never knew what time her driver might show up to take her to work. Sometimes it was quicker and less stressful just to ride her bicycle to the office.

While Kari lives and breathes the buffer, most of us have to work through certain obstacles as we begin to adopt this practice. One of the biggest stumbling blocks is a skewed misunderstanding of busyness and a deep discomfort with solitude. A lot of people would rather risk being a few minutes late than arrive early. They tell me they feel like a loser waiting alone in a restaurant or lobby. Not having enough to do means you are not keeping up with the Joneses in your productivity quotient.

The person who buffers knows when to stop and realizes that an assignment will still be there when he or she returns. Does it really matter if you squeeze in just one more phone call, text message, or e-mail before you leave? Are you that attached to your identity as a productive human being? Those who buffer realize that a little transition or "down" time is crucial to their ability to do good work. Being scheduled down to the last minute can be stressful, unhealthy, and quite possibly dangerous.

"When I am late, I am not my best self," Kari says as I glance around her home office. Windows look out over a forest of trees. On the walls hang photographs of family, one of Kari and her daughter Allison swaddled in down jackets and sitting by the ocean. A Chinese landscape depicts two birds flying across a mountain. In this setting, Kari's comment makes it clear that the buffer is about more than punctuality. It helps Kari honor her commitments to the people and tasks she cares most about.

Kari finds the buffer useful as she interacts with the outside world. "Is it possible to buffer other people," I ask?

"Of course," she says. "You lie to them about the meeting time." She says if you plan to meet someone at 2:30—someone who is always fifteen minutes late—tell her or him to meet you at 2:15. If you have a hard time getting out the door with your family, build in a half-hour buffer. It is better to take charge of departure time, accounting for predictable behavior, than chastise someone you love for being time-challenged. "Maybe it came from growing up in chaos," says Kari. "You can't control other people. You can allow for what you think will be their behavior and they can be who they are. Why put yourself in situations where you know you are going to get pissed off?"

While being early can make one look like she has nothing better to do, buffering sometimes provides unexpected benefits. Once Kari and her husband Art went to a dinner party in a new part of town. When they arrived fifteen minutes early, they decided to walk around the neighborhood. During the walk, they were able to check in with each other and enjoy their surroundings before they rang the doorbell at 6:30 P.M. At 6:50, the rest of the guests arrived with lots of excuses. Because of the buffer, Kari never worries about being late. As for the Joneses, let them race. Kari believes that having room to breathe in a schedule is more important.

Buffering can even make the difference between life and death, like the time Kari and I were driving our children back from a weekend in the mountains. Kari was at the wheel in rush-hour interstate traffic when a white Honda just ahead of us swerved out of control. As the car skidded back into traffic, a truck barreled right into the Honda's passenger side. Throughout this entire episode,

Kari never even had to slam on her brakes. She tapped them to let traffic behind us know there was trouble ahead, but was far enough behind to avoid any further accidents. She had left a buffer between our car and the ones ahead, a buffer that saved our lives.

I am the first to admit that it is hard to buffer. Is it in our nature to push things right up to the last minute? It seems like a luxury in an overcommitted life to build in time for the unexpected. Why would you complete a project with days or even hours to spare? Why be realistic about how long things actually take to finish? Because creating a little more room between activities can reduce the stress in your everyday life and help you experience glimpses of good busy.

Try it. Think about your next commitment. Whether it's your daily commute to work, going to a doctor's appointment, or meeting someone for lunch, calculate how long you think it will take to get there and then add up to one-third extra time on top. Don't give away the extra time. Have faith in the practice. See what happens.

The buffer doesn't work unless you do it. Some days I buffer and other days I forget. The difference is striking. On the days I buffer, I am happier and more generous of spirit. I am not worried about the passage of time or about being more efficient. I don't need to know what time it is every minute. I show up on time without the stress. When I buffer, I don't creep up on the car in front of me as I wait for a traffic light to turn green. I don't fret over how late I am, because I'm not late. I don't feel the urgency to fit one more thing into a busy day.

Kari is not so sure any more that she believes in a

precise formula for the buffer. She does not always set aside one-third extra time. Instead, she has become more like the cook who trusts her instincts over a recipe. While Kari does not need the formula now, we may. Many of us would like to believe that we are able to eliminate uncertainty. The buffer is a reminder that we are not in control of every circumstance in our lives, but we can be prepared.

2 Routine

Create order.

In 2000, Joe Kennedy was a successful attorney working for a prestigious corporate law firm in Pittsburgh, Pennsylvania. But after a couple of years with the firm, Joe became disheartened by his daily schedule. He was required to document his work in six-minute increments. In order to bill forty hours a week, he had to work sixty hours or more. His commitments outside of work frequently got put on hold. Friends meant a lot to Joe, but he had neither the time nor the energy to be with them.

After some deliberation, Joe did what few people do when they make good money. He quit. His law firm colleagues encouraged him to come back, and at first their appeals were tempting. But when his mom asked, "Why on earth would you do that?" Joe remembered he had quit in order to overhaul his life by finding employment that was more compatible with his commitments to family, friends, and community. Honoring his decision, Joe took a job in the non-profit sector directing an initiative called "One Kind Word," teaching store clerks how to intervene when a parent or caregiver acted abusively to a child in a store. Now his concern for children could be channeled into his professional life.

Adopting routine as a practice means creating order by following a daily schedule. Though Joe never claimed to be proficient in the practice of routine, he witnessed a remarkable colleague who was. Joe was lucky enough to work with Fred Rogers, the Emmy Award-winning children's television host. Fred was someone who modeled helpful routines on-screen and off. I travelled to Pittsburgh to hear Joe's story about Fred Rogers and his daily routines. Joe observed that, for Fred, following a routine was a way to keep his commitments to himself and others.

Joe met Fred when Fred served on the One Kind Word Advisory Board. "It was like meeting an old friend," Joe said of Mister Rogers, the only person who ever got Joe to sit still as a child. A few months after they met, Fred invited Joe to his office at WQED, the public television station in Pittsburgh, where "Mister Rogers' Neighborhood" was produced. Shortly thereafter, Fred offered Joe a job as Operations Director.

Fred's office at WQED was actually more like a kid-power clubhouse than a professional suite of offices. Emmys and other awards were unceremoniously stashed on top of cabinets. Puppets took up residence wherever they darn well pleased. The conference room was packed with reel-to-reel film and videotapes from all nine hundred episodes of "Mister Rogers' Neighborhood," framed memorabilia, and a picture of Fred on the cover of *Esquire*, November 1998.

What Joe noticed immediately after starting the job was Fred's daily routine. "Fred got up at 4:00 A.M.," Joe said. "Sometimes, I would even get e-mails at 4:00 A.M. By 7:00 A.M., he was at the Pittsburgh Athletic Association, where he swam at least a mile every day. By 9:00–9:30 A.M., he would either come into his office here or go to his writing office in a separate building. He would be in one of those two places in the morning. At noon, he would have his cup of yogurt, cheese, and crackers. Then, he would go to the other place and work."

Fred Rogers knew from experience that he operated more effectively at certain times of the day. Research about our internal body clocks confirms the benefit of a daily routine. Going to sleep and waking up at approximately the same time each day has been proven to help the insomniac get a better night's sleep. For most people, getting at least seven hours of sleep is a necessity for overall health. Eating at the same times each day helps with digestion and regularity. Fred Rogers' routine was a perfect example.

Rogers embraced routine not only in his personal life but on the television show as well, which meant, Joe told me, that Fred Rogers was the same on-screen as off. On camera, he followed a routine during each episode of "Mister Rogers' Neighborhood" that became the program's trademark. Joe said, "Each show, Mister Rogers came into the house, took off his jacket, put on the sweater and changed his shoes. The routine helped the children become ready." Mister Rogers' routine was so iconic that it became material for comedians Jim Carrey and Eddie Murphy.

Lest you think a person who follows a routine is dull, think again. Fred Rogers was the voice behind most of the puppets in the Neighborhood of Make-Believe. While Rogers was shy, his puppets gave him the courage to walk through such places as Red Square in Moscow talking to Russians through a puppet named Daniel Striped Tiger. He was not only a television celebrity, but also an authority on child development. He was often asked to testify on Capitol Hill about matters that concerned the welfare of children.

Mister Rogers' show began the same way each time. It's hard not to love a cheery guy who always bursts through a door singing "It's a Beautiful Day in the Neighborhood." The routine on the program was reliable and comforting, but left room for surprise. Mister Rogers visits a neighbor and talks with an artist, the red trolley transports viewers to the Neighborhood of Make-Believe, then we always return to see Mister Rogers feed his fish, impart a moral, or visit with Mr. McFeely, the deliveryman. The jacket would replace the sweater, and the show was over for the day.

Fred Rogers' routine, on and off the show, demonstrates that it is okay to take care of oneself before tending to the rest of the world. This kind of routine allows you to remain strong and healthy. One episode of "Mister Rogers' Neighborhood" follows Mister Rogers to his daily swim. Viewers watch as he greets the pool attendant, steps into the locker room to change, walks out to the pool, tests the water, and dives in. An underwater camera captures his pale middle-aged body and bubbling lips. Fred Rogers had nothing to hide.

I thrive on variety, chance, and serendipity. Like Joe, I grew up watching Mister Rogers demonstrate the importance of a daily routine. While I often find doing the same thing at the same time each day to be numbing, I've learned that life without routine can compromise my health. I stay up too late, eat while driving, and forget to exercise. I get stressed out over deadlines that appear out of nowhere. Routine helps me limit habits that do not serve me by setting up patterns that sustain me. A basic routine offers some assurance that I will stay in balance; there will be time to act on what's important to me. Some semblance of routine creates time for errands, assignments, and relationships that can get lost in the shuffle.

Fred Rogers did not live by six-minute increments or forty-hour balance sheets. He followed a daily routine that was both structured and flexible. This routine allowed Rogers to be busy, as busy as someone who lived by six-minute increments, but calm in his productivity. Structure liberated him to be himself. Joe scrutinized Fred's daily routine. He said, "Fred was always writing a book, a speech, or a letter. He believed every piece of correspondence—from members of the public, viewers, children or whomever—deserved a handwritten response. Fred wrote all of the scripts and music for each program. He would be looking at a script draft and would say, 'Well, what will this sound like to a blind person?'"

Following Fred did not mean mindlessly following the boss's daily routine. While Joe admired how Fred lived his life, Joe knew they were two very different people. Fred was forty years older than Joe. Fred ate yogurt and crackers. Occasionally, Joe smoked Camels and drank Diet Coke. Fred was a minister. Joe was an attorney. Joe needed less sleep than Fred, operating on five or six hours a night instead of Fred's seven or eight. When I asked Joe what he did at 4:00 A.M. every day, our conversation screeched to a halt. "Oh no, no, no, no," he said. "In the rare instances when I've actually received an e-mail at that hour, it was not because I was up early. It was because I was still up."

Fred paid attention to others even when their needs did not fit into his routine. Joe said that unless his door was closed, Fred was ready to talk. Joe and Fred frequently shared their perspectives on race and class. In the midst of his daily routine, Fred made time to talk about violence and how it affected children. Fred asked Joe questions about the Internet. There were many jokes and much laughter. A routine did not prohibit serendipity. "Oh, did you see this article?" one would ask the other. Off-screen, Rogers' routines provided his employees with a consistent schedule at work as well as reliable access to their boss.

With Fred Rogers' daily routine in mind, I plotted out my own. I decided to sleep seven to eight hours a night. I set a time to lay my head on the pillow and a time to rise. Was I going to be like Fred Rogers and go to bed at 8:00 P.M.? That was a little early. Eleven or twelve seemed more likely. Whatever I decided, I knew I would be making a small but essential commitment to my health. I then considered a structure for my days, my sixteen or seventeen waking hours. I began with meals. When did I want to eat breakfast, lunch, and dinner? What were my daily work commitments or hours? Life's curveballs could alter any routine, but having a plan made it easier to achieve a rhythm, at least for a while.

For me, balancing flexibility and specificity was crucial in establishing a routine I could embrace. Too specific a plan makes me feel claustrophobic and is doomed to failure. Fred Rogers knew exactly what he liked to eat for lunch. I would feel boxed in by prescribed meals. Fred arrived at work and left at the same times each day, but inside those boundaries, there was plenty of flexibility. I began with basics like sleeping, eating, beginning and ending work. With these simple goals, I had a chance of settling into a lasting routine.

Following a routine was not always easy for Mister Rogers. Joe remembered when he and David Newell (the on-air Mr. "Speedy Delivery" McFeely) accompanied Rogers to Washington, DC to accept an award. They were staying at a ritzy hotel. Fred wanted to eat his lunch, but refused to pay $7 for cottage cheese from room service. So he decided to go out into the neighborhood. His colleagues tried to talk him out of it because they knew what happened when Mister Rogers wandered down the street, but he insisted. "Oh, don't worry," he said, "I'm just going to go downstairs." Joe ran downstairs and caught up with him at the elevator.

They were in downtown Washington, DC by the Walter E. Washington Convention Center, and there were no stores. Still, Fred wanted his yogurt and crackers. "So we wandered up and down the street as people were doing double-takes, pointing and following us. When Fred realized he would not find his yogurt, he said, 'Let's stop in this bookstore.' Soon, there was a mob of people around us and it took over an hour to get out. Fred loved to get himself into these little situations and then say, 'I'm so surprised, can you believe that mob scene?'"

After the crowd scene and a missed nap, Joe and David were anxious when the banquet honoring Fred dragged on past 10:00 P.M. Joe knew, "Fred liked to go to bed early. Early for him was 8:00 P.M. Late for him was 8:30 P.M." Even though it was past his bedtime, Fred gave a great speech on how to inspire children's curiosity to learn. As the banquet came to a close, Joe could see that over a thousand people were about to descend on his boss. It was Joe's job to get him back to the hotel. Joe said, "Fred, if we don't leave now, you are not going to get to sleep for another two hours." That got his attention. Joe grabbed him and pushed him up the escalator. Joe said, "These people were literally chasing us saying, 'Mister Rogers, Mister Rogers.' I was tossing business cards and saying, 'We'll be sure to get back to you.' We snuck out a back door and walked back to the hotel."

After the attacks in the United States on September 11, 2001, Fred Rogers wanted to go to Qatar to explore the possibility of creating children's programs. The United States had begun its war on the Taliban in Afghanistan, and Fred Rogers wanted to create children's programs for Afghani children. "Fred wanted to go to Afghanistan and Qatar," Joe said emphatically. "I said 'Wait just a minute. You-are-not-going-over-there. We are at war.'"

Late in the summer of 2002, Fred went to his doctor to figure out why he wasn't feeling well. A round of tests determined that Fred had an aggressive form of stomach cancer and would be lucky to live a couple of months. After the diagnosis, Rogers prepared the staff to carry on without him. "Fred was quite clear that his work here was done, and he was prepared to meet his maker," Joe said. In January of 2003, Fred served as the grand marshal of the Rose Bowl Parade. He died a month later, at 2:20 A.M. on February 27, a month shy of his seventy-fifth birthday. His staff came from all over Pittsburgh in the middle of the night to gather in their conference room. In the stillness of their sorrow, the staff knew the only response Fred would have wanted was a quick return to their daily routine.

"Fred was the same man off-camera as on," Joe said. Fred told Joe how special he was just as often as he told his television audience. "This ability to treat all people— young and old, Mr. McFeely or the fan in the queue line—the same was, in my estimation, nothing short of a miracle," Joe said. "I am sure he had faults. We all do. But I don't need to hear about them. Fred Rogers seemed about as close to perfect as perfection comes. As far as I am concerned, Fred was a saint," Joe said. "He was the most spiritually centered person I have ever met."

3 Mirror
Pay attention.

"I just act like I am driving the bus, but I can hear everything that's going on behind me," Debra Westenskow said as I leaned into the aisle to hear her over the whirr of the motor. For six months, I had been a daily passenger on Debra's bus that shuttles people back and forth between Duke University and the University of North Carolina at Chapel Hill. I observed how she managed to drive the bus, take part in conversation, and be completely responsive to the environment outside the bus. She has great skill in repartee with students, staff, and faculty. Once Debra and I began to talk, the commute home became one gentle but persuasive lesson in how to pay better attention in the midst of my own busyness.

Debra has been with Duke University Transit in Durham, North Carolina since 2003. She has two grown children, whom she adores, and comes from a large family that likes to get together to party and snake around the dance floor in one long conga line. Her sister Janie is a hairstylist who fashions Debra's hair in trendy styles and colors, mostly on the red end of the rainbow. Debra is a native North Carolinian with a Southern accent whose twang is almost as evocative as the content it conveys. Before driving for Duke, she worked as a bartender, a substitute teacher, and a certified flagger for construction in Utah. For the most part, Debra has been a bus driver, someone who can just as easily manage snowstorms in Utah as college students, staff, and faculty who bend her ear about their papers, journal articles, and exams. At ease behind a large steering wheel, Debra once distinguished herself by being part of an award-winning team at a bus rodeo competition.

Sitting behind the wheel of a big bus means paying attention to everything that might go unnoticed without wide-ranging and careful scrutiny. Debra maintains constant vigilance, watching for oblivious pedestrians who walk out in front of her bus and for traffic that stops and starts at intersections. "I am focused on the two side mirrors, the width of my bus and the inside of the bus. You've always got to be in your mirrors," Debra said. Being in your mirrors is Debra's way of explaining that the bus driver must always balance her gaze backwards using the rear and side view mirrors, and forward, as she anticipates what approaches through the enormous windshield. Debra's focused attention is driven by a deep sense of responsibility for her passengers. "I have got the lives of loved ones in my hands, and I think of my own children," she said. "I would never ever risk hurting anyone on my bus. Whoever is on the bus is a part of my family."

We can all be "in our mirrors" when we figure out how to apply Debra's lessons as a bus driver to our own lives. How can you be in your mirrors? When is it important for you to pay attention to your rear and side view mirrors? How can you better anticipate the variables in your own daily life, just as Debra must predict changing stoplights, slippery roads on a rainy day, and riders running to catch the bus? Instead of focusing on your own agenda, you can learn to pay attention to the surrounding environment, as Debra has.

In my search for good busy, I struggle to balance the needs of others with my own. Debra has taught me that paying attention to the big picture is essential for a safe journey. Being in your mirrors means paying attention to the ever-changing environment as you move forward. You need to be careful not to overreact to what you observe. Instead, good busy involves being aware of possible outcomes and making small adjustments as you proceed.

It is not easy to be in your mirrors, especially when you are a bus driver, though Debra makes it sound easy. No one can maintain constant alertness. The lengthy shifts and driving back and forth on the same route can wear out the body and numb the senses. When I once rode Debra's bus for a couple of hours (just to talk), I finally lost track of where I was with all of the back and forth movement from one campus to the other. Debra admits that constantly paying attention and dealing with frequent surprises can be exhausting. She reminds me that it is important to step away from the windshield and mirrors regularly and recuperate. The lesson here is that to be able to maintain the focus necessary for work, you must step away from the responsibility periodically.

While some bus drivers limit their attention to the traffic, Debra has always made it her mission to take care of the people inside the bus as well. From years of driving university students, she is no longer surprised by the unexpected. Instead of calling the police or getting help from other drivers, Debra typically takes matters into her own hands. "A guy on the bus told his friends that he would be driving when he was drunk." While still behind the wheel, Debra said to the student, "You're not driving. I hear things, and I am normally quiet, but if it's going to hurt somebody I'll get into the middle of a conversation."

Getting into the middle of a conversation has occasionally led to conflicts. "I had a guy one night call me the 'b' word on the phone to a friend," Debra said. "I stopped the bus and said, 'Do you want me to put you off this bus?' It was so cold outside I would never have done it. I said, 'You need to sit down and be real quiet. I heard what you said. What if I was your grandmother, your sister, your aunt or your mom? Would you want someone to talk about them like that?'" The student told Debra no. Instead of exiting from the back of the bus at his stop, he walked up to the front and apologized. "Sure did," Debra said.

"I can tell you what time most people go to bed on my routes," Debra said as she drove the bus past the university president's home. While knowledge of bedtimes or details of passengers' lives may not seem related to being a safe driver, paying attention to her entire surroundings is what makes Debra a safe driver and someone who is responsive to the needs of the people around her. "I see things way before they happen. I see blinking lights and I slow way down." Unlike other bus drivers who pump the brakes down hills and in traffic, she rarely applies her own.

Debra's observational skills allow her to intervene in potentially dangerous situations. "I will scream 'watch that car' out the window of the bus when I see a pedestrian in the path of a motor vehicle." One night, Debra was driving a bus on Duke's campus. "A couple of girls got on the bus in tutus," Debra said. A few hours later, at about 3:30 A.M., another bus driver radioed Debra to tell her he saw a woman wearing a tutu walking along a dark campus road. The driver tried to get her on his bus but she refused. Debra told her fellow bus driver to follow the woman home in his bus, which he did, very slowly.

Debra's vigilance helps her to avoid disaster. During one particularly rainy evening shift, she witnessed twelve accidents. One driver attempted to pass her bus, realized he would not make it through an intersection before the red light and slammed on his brakes. The driver lost control of the car, spun around in the intersection and ran off the road. Because Debra was paying attention and responded quickly, she did not hit the spinning car with her bus. Miraculously, the other driver sustained no injury. "Someone was watching over him," Debra said. That someone was Debra.

After five years driving the shuttle between Duke and UNC-Chapel Hill, Debra was promoted to dispatcher. While she liked the pay increase and the nine-to-five schedule, she missed her time out on the road with faculty, staff, and students. "I do not want to sit behind a desk. I want to do what I enjoy. The money is good, but there is nothing like having a job that you want to go to," she said. She quit her desk job, took a pay cut, and went back to driving the bus.

4 Tunnel
Live by a metaphor.

Louisa Meacham is a revered high school teacher in Houston's inner city. A former Harvard rugby player and community organizer, Louisa comes to every moment prepared for the unexpected in the many different roles she inhabits. Louisa builds community wherever she goes through her presence, her wit, and her warmth. After she married in 1995 and took steps to start a family, her expansive life began to shrink. As the weariness of her first pregnancy took hold and the conversations began to revolve around prenatal this or that, her life seemed to be no bigger than her pregnant belly.

When her first son Joe was born in 1997, Louisa quit her teaching job. Her husband's work required that he travel all over the world, leaving Louisa with Joe and, in rapid succession, two more children. While she was grateful to have a partner who could support the family, she found that, without the satisfactions of paid work, she was often frustrated and testy. Much of Louisa's identity and self-worth had been tied to her performance in the classroom. Now her days were filled with smelly diapers, tears, play dates at the park, and the afternoon nap (if she was lucky). The day's reward was the couple of hours after the kids went to bed when she could be alone with her chores. Even though Louisa had made the decision to be at home while the kids were young (and knew it was a privilege to make this choice), it remained a daily adjustment to experience whole days when she never left the house.

One day, Louisa woke up from a dream where she was traveling through a tunnel. She was gripping a steering wheel as she drove into a tunnel through a mountain and under a harbor. The dream helped Louisa understand that she was living inside a metaphorical tunnel where her actions were bounded by a double yellow line on one side and a railing on the other. If she veered too far to the left, she risked plowing into oncoming traffic. Steering too far to the right would mean crashing into the tunnel's concrete wall.

Though Louisa's domestic dangers might seem small, the challenges of child-rearing can turn catastrophic when exhaustion impairs a caregiver's decision-making abilities. Not getting enough sleep or time alone can lead to hostility or exhaustion. When you are in the tunnel with small children, you have to figure out how to limit responsibilities and distractions so that such basic activities as sleep and personal hygiene can be accomplished. If we follow the metaphor of the tunnel, the caregiver must moderate his or her daily plans in order to get safely to the other side.

Nearly every parent I know says that while babies are a miracle, they can be demanding roommates. Babies and small children are so utterly dependent on others that a caregiver can feel constrained or even claustrophobic. After Joe was born, Louisa's world went underground. Four beings lived in her tunnel—one twenty-two-inch infant, a husband, herself, and Rosie the dog. That was it. Within a short period of time, the number of beings grew to six—three of whom were under the age of five. There wasn't room for friends or casual acquaintances. "Where did she go?" was the common refrain among the former companions and colleagues of the ever dynamic and connected Louisa Meacham. Once an avid traveler and loyal phone pal, Louisa seemed to disappear after Joe's birth. Did she get lost on the way home? When Louisa did return phone calls, she left terse messages in the middle of the day: "I'm here. Barely surviving. Love you. Mean it. Bye."

The new routine was hard on Louisa. "Sleep deprivation was a form of torture," Louisa said. "If you're not sleeping, it's hard to be excited about anything, except your next nap." For her, life in the tunnel demanded daily routine to maintain an order strong enough to stave off chaos. Year round, it was the same: breakfast at 8:00 A.M., naps at 1:00 P.M., dinner at 6:00 P.M. and lights out at 8:00 P.M. Wake up and do it again. Survival came through repetition. Children depend upon structure in their lives, even if they rebel against the enforcer. A life of limitations, one that mimics the experience of driving through a tunnel, can be more reassuring for its inhabitants than living in constant chaos.

As Louisa talked about her own tunnel, she helped me see how such a metaphor could be used in other contexts. Tunnels are periods of time during which your life is constrained by a set of fixed circumstances. A looming deadline, for instance, can send people into a tunnel. A family illness or the departure of an important colleague can make you feel like you are trapped. Recognize the tunnel. Seeing things as they are might help you feel better. At the least, you may be able to stop blaming yourself for your new limitations.

If you are traveling through one of these tunnels right now, it may feel endless, but let me assure you, the journey will come to an end. A tunnel can make even the most basic daily activities more difficult, yet more stress and anxiety come when you ignore the realities of your tunnel. Stay in your lane. People around you may expect you to carry on as if nothing has changed. But things have changed, and you can't carry on as before. Describing the tunnel to others may help them better understand your limits. While some people act as though they are perpetually in a tunnel, as though life is always too tight or too busy to be managed, in truth, most tunnels have a beginning and an end.

Because Louisa came to know her tunnel, she had advice to other tunnel travelers. First, remember the experience is finite. Do anything you can to get sleep. Be kind to your partner. Find two or three others who are in the same tunnel and talk to them, in a group if possible. "I guard my time jealously," said Louisa. In the rookie parent tunnel, your social life can revolve almost completely around other toddlers' birthday parties. "Why would I want to go to a party with thirty three-year-olds and their parents? If an activity doesn't sound fun, I don't do it," she said.

When I interviewed Louisa about her tunnel, my daughter and son were five and three years old, respectively. I resonated with Louisa's words, because I was driving right behind her in the same lane. I hadn't had a good night's sleep in several years and had limited my professional life so I could be with my kids during the day. I struggled with some of the issues of ego, no health insurance, and the limited financial resources that came with cutting back on paid work. Years later, I continue to experience some of the confines of the parenthood tunnel, even though my children are more independent every day. I am grateful to have gained a metaphor and a practice from Louisa that helps me to believe that any difficult phase in life may not be permanent.

When her three kids were out of diapers, Louisa could see glimmers of the tunnel's end. Her former colleagues were calling her to come back to her job as a high school teacher. Dutifully, and with some initial excitement, she returned their calls. But on the night before an interview, all three kids got sick. It was a sign she was not yet out of her tunnel. A headhunter presented another job opportunity, but that same day, Joe was bitten by a caterpillar and screamed in pain until three A.M. No, not ready yet.

While she was in the tunnel, people who were farther down the pike than Louisa gave her hope. She felt excitement when others joined her, such as when a neighbor who had been trying to have a baby for six years became pregnant and gave birth. As Louisa came closer and closer to the end of her tunnel, the experience began to look more like a cocoon. With her youngest in elementary school, she returned to teaching high school. The tunnel she drove into with the birth of Joe had come to an end.

There can be comfort in knowing the parameters of your tunnel. Keep faith you will get to the other end. Louisa now makes it her mission to help people who live outside the parenting tunnel understand how to interact with the weary souls still inside. First, "feed and love them." Then tell them they are not boring (even if all they do is talk about drool). When you call, always ask, "Is this a good moment for you?" If the parent does the dishes as you talk, don't be offended. Doing two things at once is often required. Finally, use email or text. That way a parent can communicate even if their children are screaming in the background.

Try to remember some of your own experiences with tunnels. Are you like me and feeling a little claustrophobic or enclosed? Are you like me and feeling the exhilaration of moving through an engineering feat that allows you to drive under water? Have you traveled on foot through tunnels such as the ones in a subway system? Keep these images in mind as you think about your life right now. Are you constricted by your commitments? Do you feel limited in your options? Would you like to turn around but feel like you have to keep moving forward? Are you like Louisa and having a hard time even getting out the door? If any of these questions apply, you may be living in the tunnel.

The beauty of the tunnel metaphor is that once you recognize where you are, you can settle into the new reality. Getting through a tunnel is a test of patience and endurance. While inside the tunnel, the variables may not change much. You will have a limited range of motion. You will not be able to change your lane, but you will get out eventually. Your job is to keep moving forward. This tunnel shall pass.

5 Sliver

Move beyond procrastination.

Tom Rankin is a well-known photographer, professor, and director of the Center for Documentary Studies (CDS) at Duke University. He works in a majestic old house nestled by the railroad tracks in Durham, North Carolina. CDS is a hive of activity related to documentary films, audio recordings, and still photographs. Before we began our conversation, I sat down in a rocking chair by Tom's desk as he wrote one last e-mail. With cathedral ceilings and small windows, his office was bathed in soft natural light. The desk and couch were covered with piles of papers and books. A crucifix made of beer bottle caps and a painting of Muhammad Ali hung on the walls along with a variety of posters. Slide carousels perched on top of piles of administrative memos. An old water bottle and vitamins languished on the floor behind the desk chair.

Tom wears some of the stress of the job on his face, but his energy and smile make him appear younger than his years. A native of Louisville, Kentucky, he carries the accent with him. As we talked, Tom sat beside his computer screen with one arm over the top, leaning forward to make a point. "The next book you write will be about neatness and then I will clean up my office," he said, grinning as he surveyed his cluttered space.

While Tom is an award-winning photographer, I dare say no one has ever sought out his time management advice. I wanted to know Tom's secret. He is an active and published photographer who manages a large staff and several documentary projects at once. Surely he multitasks. Perhaps he takes pictures of staff meetings or photographs architectural details of the building. But no. Instead of trying to be both artist and administrator at once, Tom appears to focus on one task or role at a time. Listen to his language and you hear one word over and over. Instead of multitasking or following time-saving techniques, Tom lives by the sliver.

A sliver is an increment of time in which Tom tackles something he has put off. He drops everything and slivers. Essential to the practice is being able to set aside pressing demands from the outside world and do one thing. Accepting the challenge of the sliver means not only engaging in a postponed activity, but also suspending worry over any responsibilities left behind. Tom's slivers can last five minutes or five hours or five days.

As both professor and artist, Tom has always tried to live in areas where good photo opportunities were close by. After time in Atlanta, he took a job at Delta State University in Mississippi and fell in love with the state. A few years later, he moved his family to Oxford to teach at Ole Miss. Landscapes and barns, rivers and rusting objects far away from four-lane highways were his métier. Daylight brought definition to his images, not the flash of the camera or the blink of a fluorescent light. After Tom became an administrator at Duke, his photography was all but squeezed out by his everyday responsibilities.

The sliver is how Tom makes art and finds time for rejuvenation in the midst of his daily administrative life. He looks at the calendar page full of meetings and conference calls, takes a deep breath, and begins to carve out the slivers. He slivers out a day or two here and there, sometimes even a week or two, where he sets aside his administrative chores for his own personal photography or other activities that matter to him. Sometimes he walks the halls of CDS to catch up with employees. Instead of waiting for the next staff meeting or scheduled review, these visits are opportunities for Tom to take the pulse of his team. Tom slivers out time to keep in touch.

Tom never defined his sliver strategy. It was only after I reviewed notes from our conversation that I discovered the word sliver written all over my notebook. Tom said he slivered time to photograph, to eat lunch, or to tackle tedious work projects. While Tom's slivers seemed to address what he wanted to do, I began to use the sliver as an approach to assignments in my life that I dread. When I do not feel like returning a phone call or doing the dishes at ten o'clock at night, I say the word "sliver" to push myself into action. Surely, I can do just about anything for ten minutes, I tell myself. I stand up. I put on shorts and

I exercise. I step into the sliver and do something I probably would have put off or never done at all. After I finish a postponed activity, I almost always hear myself saying, "Well, that wasn't so bad," or "I think I will sliver again tomorrow."

When Tom took over at CDS, he could no longer leave work for a few days at a time to focus on a photography project. He has learned, however, to make room for his art in the midst of the "frenetic and random" responsibilities of being an administrator. His perspectives about life have been informed by his time as a photographer. With a border around an intention, it is far more likely to happen. "Framing renders anything closer," Tom said as he thought about his own daily life. Framing that very good intention is what Tom does each time he slivers. When you sliver, you determine what fits in your life instead of leaving it up to chance.

Beginning a perfunctory task or a creative endeavor is the perilous part. The sliver provides a bridge to get started. Once inside the sliver, I watch my mind and body forget whatever seemed to get in the way earlier. I always stay in the sliver longer than I imagined I would when I was still in the dreading phase.

Giving away the sliver is the number one reason it does not happen. You give the sliver away when you think there is not time in your day to tackle an assignment that does not seem urgent or immediately relevant. You give away the sliver when the time you imagine it will take to accomplish your intention seems impossible to fit into your tight schedule.

Tom needs to carve out time alone. He doesn't thrive without it. Carving out time to be in the darkroom, whether he gets things done or not, is a necessity for Tom's peace of mind. "I don't always know when I go in there what I am going to do. I don't go into the darkroom because someone asks me to go there at nine o'clock in the morning. A lot of people, including myself, find it much easier to fill the day than to discern what the day should be. You just react. Work does that for people," Tom said.

"Do you think time is a controlled substance in our country?" Tom asked as he mused over his own life and obligations. Later when I got home, I read up on "controlled substances" and found lists of narcotics and other prescription drugs. The more I pored over these lists, the more I understood Tom's query. Just like cocaine or valium users, we crave more time than we can get legally.

"We all have excuses for why we don't have any time," Tom said, as he pondered his own strategy of the sliver. "It's nine o'clock in the morning, and I have to be doing something," he said of our societal norm. "But you don't have to be doing something. It's a response to perceived or real pressure from the outside," he said.

Sometimes we put things off and blame the busyness or the constraints within our everyday work life. The lesson behind the sliver is that you can carve out time for what matters to you by setting a goal, putting time limits around it, and acting on your intentions.

When we sliver, we flex our ability to be proactive in the middle of our daily reactivity. The increment of time does not matter as much as the fact that you actually use the time to engage in the chosen activity. You will give your sliver away to no one with the possible exception of a sick child or a national emergency. Let the sliver whisk you away from your daily routine to engage in acts of rejuvenation and passion. While not all slivers are comfortable or easy, you are likely to feel better in the end.

6 **Geological**
Take the long view.

Alexander X. Byrd, Associate Professor of History at Rice University in Houston, Texas, understands his daily life as a timeline. Instead of focusing on the time on his watch, he lives by what he calls "geological time." For Alex, his own life is but a blip on the screen compared to the many eras of Mother Earth. If he gets fired from his job, so what? It will not register in this Cenozoic era. He has learned how to build his life around what gives him joy because all the rest will be forgotten. Even though Alex lives in an era of speed and pressure, he takes his time. "Why the rush?" he wonders of the world around him. Alex has learned how to be geological in his approach to everyday life.

Alex is about six feet tall, wears glasses, and shaves his head. He takes life pretty seriously. His voice quakes when he makes a point that matters to him. When he is comfortable and relaxed, he is generous in his laughter and his goofiness. While being geological may appear to be plodding, Alex's career has been nothing short of remarkable. Alex took eleven years to get his PhD from Duke University. He is now a tenured faculty member at Rice. In 2009, he won the Wesley-Logan Prize from the American Historical Association for his book, *Captives and Voyagers: Black Migrants across the Eighteenth-Century British Atlantic World*. In 2010, he won the Douglass Adair Memorial Award for the best article published in a particular academic journal over the previous six years. His research has changed in recent years to focus on life in the urban South since the 1954 *Brown vs. Board of Education* ruling that racial segregation in educational facilities was a violation of the United States Constitution's Fourteenth Amendment.

I can barely remember life without Alex as my friend. We met when he was a sophomore at Rice and I was just out of college. Alex helped to establish the Rice Student Volunteer Program (RSVP) that continues to serve the needs of residents in the greater Houston community. I was a "road warrior" at the time, working for a national organization named the Campus Outreach Opportunity League (COOL) that helped hundreds of universities develop ways to give back to their surrounding communities through academic and student life programs. Alex was given the charge of creating the mission statement for their endeavors with RSVP. Both Alex and his wife Jeanette, a school principal, lead by example. When I decided to go in search of good busy, I knew I had to talk with Alex.

Even though Alex is a historian, Alex employs a geological metaphor to make daily choices. The father of two young children, Alex gave up reading the newspaper until his children were in kindergarten. "What matters is the whole span of your life, not the one or two things you do or don't do now," Alex said. You can live by this perspective too when you learn how to tell time geologically. Even though Alex is a tenured professor at a prestigious institution, he reminds himself daily that he cannot keep up with the speed that is expected of him. He is slow, he said, and as much as he has tried to change over the years, he has stayed the same. "Any thought counts as work," Alex said.

Is there anything good about being slow, I asked? "I don't know if there is anything good about it, but I am slow. People all over the world are faster than I am," he said. "My mom is late and slow. My boy has gotten his grandma's slowness. You should see us when we are together, the boy and I. There's nothing bad about it. I miss deadlines. I just keep writing. Jeanette is always hurrying me along," Alex said.

"People expect me to be as efficient and productive as possible and speed is a part of the equation," Alex said. He reminds his colleagues that he is not at his best when he rushes to meet deadlines without spending time with God and his family. Anxiety creeps in when life is managed by minutes instead of months and years. In setting his watch to geological time, Alex often finds the peace necessary to show up at his desk and write without the fear or pressure of unrealistic deadlines.

Geological time means seeing your entire life. You look for what matters and try to forget the rest. As a historian, Alex says he is a reader of "dead people's mail." Every day, he travels back four or five hundred years to enter the world of people he brings to life again through his writing. Alex's research shapes him. He realizes how little is actually passed down through the ages. In response, Alex narrows his own goals for himself and simply hopes to "see my children go to elementary school, die married, and go to heaven." In the next breath, he adds, "Write the book before the tenure process is finished."

Alex's words are measured as we talk on the telephone. I wonder how often people make up their responses to my questions, in contrast to the countless times Alex just says, "I don't know." While I appreciate his honesty, I am unnerved, until I realize that geological time honors the unknown more than having the "right" answer. Alex searches for answers, not always expecting they will appear.

Alex's father was born to an African-American soldier and a white German woman, adopted by an African-American couple, and raised by them in the United States. Once, while living in London, Alex decided to go to Germany to meet his birth grandmother. Even after Alex discovered she had died, he and his wife traveled to his birth grandmother's hometown and visited a great-aunt in a nursing home. When Alex called his father from the nursing home, his father wept. Alex knows some moments in life are painful in the short term. In geological time, it is far more important to wrestle with and make peace with difficult situations than to avoid them. When Alex's father died a few years later, there was solace in the memory of that cathartic phone call.

As an academic, Alex gained perspective from slave ship logs he studied for research he conducted on the history of the African Diaspora. As he pored over the records of thousands of people who were transported to Jamaica, the West Indies, and the United States, he realized that names of individual slaves had not been recorded in the logbooks. The most basic identity markers—name, home, family lineage, or occupation—were irrelevant in the slave trade. Through his archival work, Alex realized that even one's own identity will probably be erased in geological time. Any evidence of our walk here on Earth, in bondage or in freedom, can eventually be lost.

As a professor, Alex brings the lessons learned from his research and everyday life into the classroom. He encourages his students to embrace geological time. "What do you want to look back on?" Alex asks. "They focus semester to semester. What a waste," Alex says. He encourages his students to see the big picture.

To embrace the metaphor of geological time in your own life, write down your top three or four goals in life. Remember, Alex's are to see his children go to elementary school, die married, go to heaven, and write his book. If we keep our lists front and center, we are freed up to claim what sustains us. A big part of experiencing the good in one's commitments is realizing that hopes, goals, and dreams take time to accomplish. When my kids have been sick for two weeks with no sign of relief, I try to keep in mind that in geological time their ailments will be forgotten.

You can live by geological time as well. Just as Alex lives by the goals of being a "decent dad, decent husband, and a good Baptist man," you can create your own goals. When you do, your watch will be set to geological time. And in this scale of time defined not by seconds or minutes but by tectonic shifts, volcanic action, and evolution, you can determine what's most important to you. Experiencing time through a metaphor means coming up with an image that best describes your current daily existence. Whether it is a tunnel, a mountain, or something else, the image you adopt can provide some perspective and limits to your everyday life. Your job is to pay attention to the fact that your own life is short, though the universe may go on forever.

7 Sequence
Make a playlist.

Shawn Amos is a songwriter, musician, singer, pop culture commentator, digital industry leader, and record producer in Los Angeles, California. He sits on the board of trustees of the Rock and Roll Hall of Fame and Museum and has produced hundreds of music and comedy compilations. He uses a metaphor of the short-order cook to describe his ability to meet the tightest of deadlines. Although he keeps a frenetic pace and describes himself as hyperactive, Shawn maintains order by making lists.

In the three years we were in regular communication, I experienced these lists as efficiently expressed e-mails and to-the-point telephone conversations. Each time I called, he answered briskly, "This is Shawn," put me on hold for about a minute to finish the previous call or assignment, and then returned for conversation. One of Shawn's gifts is his ability to take an assemblage of discrete items such as songs, events, poems, and daily chores and put them in a particular order that allows him to create a new experience or move a project forward.

This ordering process is what I call Shawn's ability to sequence. He holds the disparate pieces of his life together by recording ideas, plans, and tasks on paper, screen, or heart and then commits himself to action. Put simply, Shawn knows how to sequence activities in a creative process like no other human being I have ever met.

Shawn bridges worlds that are difficult to span in the music business. As a black artist who records in such varied musical genres as country, soul, and pop, he often appeals to white performers and listeners. People who are bound by the limitations of genre do not realize that a diversity of sounds and musical traditions can flourish together. As a result, Shawn continues to wrestle with a music industry that seeks to label his music too narrowly.

Shawn is married to Marta Martin, a film and television actor. When I first visited Shawn, he and Marta had one child, two-year-old Piper; they soon added two more. The plans Shawn makes have to include a wife who travels for her work and the needs of young children. When I heard Shawn in concert in 2004 and later spent a "typical" day with him in Los Angeles, I watched him weave these disparate commitments into his own brand of good busy.

On the morning I visited Shawn in his apartment, he was transforming his living space into a recording studio so that he could record the title track on an album. He introduced me to the family mutt Mimi and got back to work. While Shawn sat at his mixing board trying to resolve a technical difficulty, I retired to the burgundy couch across from a mantle full of family photographs.

Shawn lost his mother, Shirlee Ellis Amos, in 2003. After a lifelong struggle with schizoaffective disorder, she took her own life. While sorting through her things, Shawn found programs, proof sheets, and portfolio shots from his mom's music career. As he grieved for his mom, he decided to create a sequence of songs to commemorate her life. A week after his mom died, Shawn penned the words to the title track of his album, "Thank You Shirl-ee May." He spent the next ten months writing songs and creating musical sequences from his raw emotions, trying to make sense of his mother's life, one track at a time.

About an hour after I arrived at Shawn's, Clint the technician showed up. Then Ben the guitar player arrived, his wild red hair looking as if he had just gotten out of bed. The task for the morning was to add Ben's guitar to the title track, "Thank You Shirl-ee May." When Ben asked why I was there, I told him I was interested in how people cope with busyness. "You can tell I don't know how to deal," Ben responded. "The number six doesn't even work on my cell phone."

After the recording session, Shawn and I drove across town to Shout! Factory, the entertainment company where he worked. The company produced music compilations, live shows, documentaries, and television shows. It was a place where Shawn could make good use of his ability to put items in just the right order. On albums he has recorded and projects he has produced, he knows how to identify the beginning, middle, and end of a story in order to demonstrate that a sum can express a greater meaning than any of its individual parts. One of Shawn's projects exemplified his practice of sequencing for me.

While previously working for Rhino Records, Shawn went to see a Harlem Renaissance exhibit at the Los Angeles County Museum of Art. Somewhere between the paintings and the poetry, Shawn's mind came alive with possibility. What if he produced a box set to accompany the exhibit? Without hesitating, he made a list. He would ask the curator for permission to proceed, pitch the project to his colleagues at Rhino, run financial projections, and try to convince the higher-ups that the project would provide good material for public relations.

Shawn had to consider all the Rhino departments. "You want the marketing people to see the idea so they can envision selling it to the media. You want the salespeople to envision selling it to retailers. You want the finance people to believe you can do it cheaply so there is not a big investment up front. You have to convince three parties for three different reasons."

Once Rhino signed onto the project, the pace of Shawn's work only escalated. He decided to portray this remarkable period of the 1920s and 1930s by alternating tracks of spoken word and music. He asked African-American artists Quincy Jones and Coolio to read essays and poetry from the Harlem Renaissance in between musical tracks such as "Ain't Misbehavin'" and "Saint Louis Blues."

He built a "brain trust of academics" and consulted with each one about what music and literature to include. He reserved tracks for "obvious" musicians such as Duke Ellington and Cab Calloway. "You have to have the hits," he said, "the people who may not be household names, but are clearly acknowledged figures of that period. Then you want a few cool surprises." Shawn's ability to tell a coherent story through a sequence of carefully arranged tracks was his gift to the project. He knew which essays to put beside which songs and which performing artist should read which pieces.

Shawn did not want the celebrities to say they were too busy to participate, so he came up with a strategy to record their spoken tracks in the midst of their daily lives. Shawn met August Wilson, the Pulitzer Prize-winning playwright, in Wilson's hotel room in New York just before lunch. He met Darius Rucker, the lead singer of the popular band Hootie and the Blowfish, backstage and recorded Rucker before he went on stage. Shawn recorded Branford Marsalis, the jazz and classical saxophonist, in Marsalis' attic one morning before he took his kids to school, and actor Angela Bassett recorded just before she made dinner for her family. Shawn figured out how to complete the project by adapting his imagined sequence to the daily commitments of his collaborators.

Once the tracks were recorded, Shawn had to get the rights to use the music and texts, then work with graphic designers on the packaging. Shawn described the process. "What's the cover going to look like? What about the box set? What about the booklet? What kind of essays? What photos? Wouldn't it be cool if we had some art? 'Oh, I have a painting that has never been published before,' Rick Powell told me. Let's put a timeline and drop in a whole booklet of key Renaissance events." At the end, "you sequence the thing and master it, making sure all of the levels are even between tracks. Maybe you want a little bit more of a space between the end of 'Downhearted Blues' by Bessie Smith and the beginning of August Wilson for dramatic effect. It has to be a consistent listen from beginning to end. Then, the finished product goes to market."

Knowing how to create and follow a sequence in our daily lives does not come naturally to all of us. Some people lack the attention span, the time, or the foresight to create and follow a plan from start to finish. Following a sequence requires being brave enough to carry out our intentions to the very end. It's about proceeding step by step to realize a larger vision. Sequences do not have to be complicated or deep. They can be as simple as making a grocery list or learning how to be a salsa dancer. Often, it is that first step that can elude us. One, two, three, here we go.

In my conversations with Shawn, I discovered that sequences do not have to be rigid or hierarchical. When he produces a music compilation, he is not thinking about which song is the very best, but is considering which songs will work best together and what order will create the most satisfying listening experience.

Shawn's use of sequences isn't limited to the workplace. He engages them in his domestic routines as well. One of our conversations began with a discussion of his daily routine. "I get up between 4:00 and 5:00 in the morning and need at least two hours to myself. I'm in my living room and it's dark. If my daughter Piper didn't get up so early in the morning, I would do the same drill in the middle of the night. When my daughter gets up, I'm the one who gets her ready for school," he said.

Days of the week are never just Monday, Tuesday, or Wednesday to Shawn—they have names and themes such as Piper's day, rehearsal night, or date night with Marta. When he travels, there is a routine as well. "Now that Piper is a little older," Shawn said, "I try really hard to explain what my business trips are about before they happen. Then I call at least once a day, but preferably twice."

Shawn's father is Wally Amos or "Famous Amos," the chocolate chip cookie magnate. Shawn warned me early that if I wanted to try to understand him, I had better talk with his dad. When I reached Wally by telephone at his home in Hawaii, I realized how similar Shawn and Wally are. Both work in the business world and are also extremely community-minded. Both care deeply for the welfare of other people and do so by contributing their own time and talents to causes in which they believe. Wally has been the chief spokesperson for a literacy project, while Shawn has been involved in a theatre group that works with at-risk kids and served on the board of a suicide prevention organization. Even though their lives have been so different from one another, each has an abiding respect for the other's accomplishments.

Shawn is the only child of Wally's second marriage. He has two brothers and a sister from two other marriages. Everyone in the family turns to Shawn to make order out of chaos. When things go wrong, Shawn is usually the one who gets the call for help. While he does not relish the role, he knows he is the one who can launch a sequence of actions under stress.

While sequencing can be useful in many situations, it also has its liabilities. It can be difficult for people who depend upon lists to live in the moment. Any present joy can be obscured by worries or plans for the future or by the next item on the sequence. "I went to a birthday party for one of Piper's friends, and all of the adults were on cell phones," Shawn said. "We were all coming together for an occasion, but no one was really there. Everyone always had one foot in and one foot out as we multitasked ourselves into a stupor. I'm guilty of it too."

At the end of the afternoon I spent with Shawn at Shout!, it was time to pack up and leave before he felt his work was done. But done it had to be, because the babysitter was with Piper at home, his wife Marta was on an acting assignment in Florida, and it was time to be Dad.

"Let's make a plan, dude," Shawn said to Piper as we settled in back at his home. "You can play with your Pooh blocks, watch some of *Yellow Submarine* or . . . ?" He hesitated to see what Piper might add. The daddy sequence was in motion. With no response, a tickle session began. "Did you eat your banana at school today?" Shawn asked. "No, I threw it away," Piper said with a sly smile. "Well, that's not good to waste food," Shawn said as he set up the table for her dinner.

After Shawn helped Piper to bed, he returned to the living room to see if I wanted some green tea. Since it was 9:30 at night, I figured this tea was probably going to be our dinner. Meals appeared to be optional on Shawn's playlist that day. I was hungry, but I was also amazed that he did not appear to suffer any loss of energy from missing lunch and dinner. Over tea, we talked about what drives Shawn to make and follow sequences. "Every day, I want to get up and do something that gets me closer to where

I want to be," he said. "At the end of the day, if I've done that, then it is a good day. I thrive on activity and I thrive on having a lot of things going on at once. If there's a little bit of room for something, anything, I will fill it. That's the way I was from day one."

Around eleven, Shawn and I said good-night and I made my way toward Piper's bed, the one she had vacated for me. As I lay in this child's room, illuminated by city lights undeterred by blinds, I thought about the day. Shawn had demonstrated that while making lists invites a beginning, learning how to turn a list into a sequence enables further progress. Sequencing pushes intentions into motion—but not that night. I slid a big pile of Piper's stuffed animals over to the corner of the bed, crawled under the sheets, and let the pulse of the day move through me like a sequence into sleep.

8 **Gungee**

Keep going.

Esther was eighteen years old in 1979 and madly in love with a Native American rodeo star, a quiet, bashful man named Richard, who was ten years older and a nationally ranked team roper on the Indian Rodeo circuit. Soon after they were married, she gave birth to Dustin, their first and her only child. Though she had long planned to escape Klamath Falls, Oregon by becoming a fashion buyer or a flight attendant, by the time Dustin was a toddler, Esther realized that becoming a wife and mother had derailed her plans. After Esther discovered that her rodeo-riding husband was fooling around with other women when away on the rodeo circuit, she asked for a divorce and moved seventy miles away from their hometown.

But seventy miles was not far enough. Richard would come looking for Esther when he was drunk or high, had a lady on his arm, or all of the above. Whenever he showed up, Esther felt what she described as Gungee, an icky sensation that welled up from deep inside her. It was an experience she compared to riding on a plane for days. "When you're so tired and you never feel clean and you never eat right and you never get enough sleep, that's Gungee," she said. Instead of obsessing over the Gungee, you do what you can to adapt and keep going.

Gungee is the practice of recognizing that there is hardship in life that we can't control. We never know how long Gungee's effect on our psyche will last—or its impact on our ability to move forward in our lives. The only thing we can do is tell ourselves every day that we need to keep going in spite of whatever struggles or injustices (may exist). When something bad happens or our mood shifts to a dark place, we can recognize that we are experiencing Gungee.

Like sizzle, crunch, and snap, the word Gungee sounds like its meaning. Gungee means working a third shift, only to move on to the next job a few hours later. Living with constant uncertainty or fear is Gungee. Esther's Gungee was about raising her son near his father but without his father's help, in an economically depressed part of Oregon, and just barely getting by. Esther could either endure life in Klamath Falls, or she could make a change.

One day, Esther ran into a friend from the nearby reservation who was moving to Las Vegas for work and said she could catch a ride. That was a Wednesday. On Friday, she put her belongings in storage, got in her friend's car with her son, and they drove the 871 miles to Vegas. "I cried the whole way," she later recalled. Though Esther hoped the move would mean a better life for Dustin and distance from her ex-husband, there were no assurances.

At the time, Las Vegas, Nevada and Atlantic City, New Jersey were the only two places in the United States where gambling was legal. Though she had never imagined working in a casino, Esther got a job running Keno at Circus Circus and became an instant success. Soon, however, she discovered how difficult it was to work so closely with people's money, their fantasies, and their desire to have a good time away from home. The excesses of that world, the constant tin-tin-tin sound of the gambling machines, and the flaring tempers wore her down. Gungee had followed her to Las Vegas.

Esther quit Circus Circus and took a job as a blackjack dealer at another establishment. "I thought working in a casino as a blackjack dealer would be glamorous, but the people were rude," she said. The negative energy at the casino was as bad as the hopelessness she had witnessed back in Oregon. In moving to Las Vegas, Esther had hoped to escape the endless cycle of poverty, the emotional pain, and the Gungee, but she hadn't. She decided to leave casino work and look for other employment.

She got a job as a bartender at the Sunrise Lounge. Having tended bar in Klamath Falls, she knew what to expect. There would be gambling at the bar, but there would be nothing like the volume or the stress she had experienced at the casino. Although her graveyard shift and the clientele were not always ideal, Esther was able to hire a woman to babysit for Dustin and to get home in time to cook his breakfast before school. With no child support, Esther wound up having to get a second job babysitting during the day to make ends meet. She was so tired from working day and night that her boss started picking her up for work just to make sure she got to the bar on time. "We didn't have a phone," she said.

Esther built a group of loyal patrons who followed her all over town when she changed jobs and worked at other bars. People came to her bar because they admired her. They sought her counsel on matters of the heart, child-rearing, and life choices. Esther's appeal came from deep inside. She helped people understand that the secret was not learning how to eliminate hardships but how to tame your Gungee. Esther helped people build the stamina to deal with their Gungee.

Recognizing and moving beyond your Gungee does not mean turning into Pollyanna. Yes, there is deep pain and suffering in the world. The challenge is to figure out how to keep moving forward. If Gungee surrounds you right now, describe it to yourself. Estimate when it began. Describe the circumstances that brought it on. How does it affect you each day? Whether it is exhaustion, depression, or lack of focus, describe how the Gungee is taking a toll on you. Once you have described it, consider what you can do to keep perspective until the Gungee abates.

I met Dustin, Esther's son, in 2003 when my husband and I served as residence hall parents at Union College in Kentucky. A compact but strong young man, he played every position on the offensive and defensive line of the college football team. Though he seemed somewhat out of place in Appalachia with his short-cropped hair, dark brown eyes, and 702 (the Las Vegas area code) tattooed on one bicep, he made himself at home. We always sat near the football team in the dining hall, and it was easy to see that Dustin was often at the center of their conversations. When I got to know him, I marveled at all he could do, balancing classes, jobs, and sports. He is the only person I have ever known who could dress up as Santa Claus for kids in town and then suit up in an orange and black football uniform and be ready to tackle the opposition on the same day. When I asked him how he did it all, he said, "I do a lot more with what God gave me." When we talked, Dustin often mentioned his mom, the bartender in Las Vegas.

As a boy, Dustin spent his summers working on his grandmother's farm in Oregon; when he was ten, he refused to go home at the end of the summer. Why walk to the bus stop in Las Vegas when you can drive your own tractor in Klamath Falls? His desire left Esther in a bind. What do you do when the person you love most asks you to move back into the middle of your Gungee? She moved back to Klamath Falls, but never unpacked, returning to Vegas in less than a month. All the things that had stirred up her Gungee in the first place were still there. People were broke, miserable, and "wanted to drag her down," as Dustin characterized his mom's feelings.

Although Dustin loved being on the farm and back near his roots, his own Gungee stirred every time he interacted with his father. Dustin's deep bass voice fell to a hush when he spoke of his dad. "I love him. I just don't know him that well. In Oregon, I can remember him coming to see me only twice. I remember countless times he was going to come get me and he didn't come. I was twelve or thirteen when he did it the last time. My grandpa said my dad was not going to hurt me again." Soon after that, he moved back to Las Vegas.

Esther and Dustin didn't have a traditional mother-and-son relationship. Their bond was more of a working partnership. "Dustin was all I ever had," Esther said, "and most of the time, he was my buddy. We always did everything together. It's like we grew up together. If he ever got in trouble, he would always say, 'Mom, we have to talk.' He was never afraid to tell me anything." The Gungee they faced, as a single parent and her son, was often held at bay in the strength of their relationship.

For Senior Day at Union College, the parents of a fellow football player sent Esther a plane ticket so she could attend. While she was grateful for their generosity, the stark contrast between her life and the lives of the other parents presented her with yet another Gungee. "They have everything," she said. "At the game, they'd ask me, 'Oh, so you bartend in Las Vegas?' And of course they're interested because people are fascinated with Las Vegas, but then on the other hand, I'm looking at them and I'm thinking, God, I want what you have. I've failed at two marriages, and I couldn't give my son the best of everything. I should have looked ahead more, and I should have focused on going to school to make a career for myself. Then again, I look at people who have problems with their kids and they have everything, and they are asking *me* what to do."

While Dustin loved playing football, he worried about his mom. "I worry about basic things. She deals with drunks all of the time. I worry about someone beating her up or about her getting robbed in the parking lot," he said. "I definitely do not want to live with my mom," Dustin clarified, "I'm sure my mom would tell you the same thing." But he also did not like being 2,000 miles away.

Many of us try to ignore or rush past our Gungee. The impulse makes sense. Why wouldn't you want to move beyond the haze and discomfort you feel? But this desire to move beyond the Gungee too quickly is a mistake. There is no quick fix. Instead, listen to what the Gungee is trying to tell you. But don't wait for your dilemmas and dramas to be resolved to make the next move.

Even if Gungee goes away, it can come back later. Our responsibility is to get stronger and smarter in how we respond to it. While you cannot will it away, you can learn to deal with it. Dealing with it may mean making modest adjustments to your daily schedule. It may mean getting more sleep or working less if you can. When your life is out of balance, it's an invitation for Gungee to take hold.

Years passed. Life got better for both Dustin and Esther. Dustin grew up and got married. Esther traded the graveyard shift for more reasonable hours. With a better schedule, regular customers and bigger tips, the Gungee slowly subsided. After talking with Esther on the phone for several months, I decided to visit her in Las Vegas. After visiting Shawn Amos in Los Angeles, I drove through a desert lit up with neon to meet Esther. Around ten that night, I arrived at Esther's bar, The Big Inning. It took no time to recognize her. There she was behind a huge butterfly-shaped bar, relaxed and talking with customers. Fourteen televisions, all set to different sports programs, glowed above her head. ESPN pennants and an inflated football bobbed around in the breeze from a vent. Images of sports legends—Tony Dorsett, Ken Griffey Jr., Wayne Gretsky, Barry Bonds, and Troy Aiken—graced the walls. Esther had an hour left in her shift.

Even on a busy Friday night, Esther took time with regulars and newcomers alike to find out how they were doing. When a customer announced, "I just bought a convertible from Oklahoma off of eBay," she ran outside to examine the new car. She returned saying, "What a big-ass steering wheel," imitating the steering motion. After her shift, we went to Esther's apartment, in one of about twenty complexes situated along a palm tree-lined road. Once inside, Esther dumped out her purse and counted $700 in tips, her pay for the night. Was it all worth it, she wondered aloud?

Dustin had become a high school football and wrestling coach and physical education teacher. Esther had her real estate license and had fallen in love with a high school classmate. While Esther's Gungee was not completely at bay, she found peace in knowing that her son was married and doing well professionally. Even though she struggled to make ends meet sometimes, her life had promise. "No one else is going to take care of you," Esther said.

At 1:00 A.M., we both went to bed. I slept in Dustin's room, a mother's shrine to a son who lived far away. There were two sepia portraits of Dustin and his dad in Western motif with rifles and long cowboy coats, several football shots, baseball and football trophies, and a Mile 72 highway marker in honor of Dustin's football number. Esther and Dustin's music was stored together in his room and ranged from Country Western musician Garth Brooks to R & B artist Usher.

Lying in bed, I thought about some of my own Gungee. I remembered previous bouts of illness when I made matters worse by obsessing over bad things that could happen next. I considered failures that prompted me to give up on an assignment instead of just taking a break and returning to the work later. I conjured up moments of paralyzing fear, the result of Gungee that would have passed had I been more patient. I fell asleep in Las Vegas that night grateful for a bartender and new friend who was gently guiding me toward good busy by teaching me that hardship can be endured, even if it never completely goes away.

9 Milk (your cows)

Reckon with your responsibilities.

When I got off the commuter flight in Akron, there was no mistaking Tom Spuhler. At 6'2", he was the guy in the waiting crowd with cat whisker wrinkles, leathery skin, and a bushy handlebar mustache. As we walked toward the airport exit, I noticed that Tom gestured with his entire body. His elbows, knees, and chin helped his hands tell a story. Since Tom is a dairy farmer, I expected to find a mud-splattered truck waiting for us in the parking lot. Instead he directed me to his red Corvette. Tom is a twenty-first century farmer.

Tom's livelihood depends on his cows, hundreds of them. Because he understands what it means to be responsible for hundreds of udders that cannot wait, even in the event of a family emergency, he became the inspiration for the practice I call milk (your cows). My visit with Tom helped me realize that we all have dependents in our lives—the animals, plants, and people who need us. While I do not have the responsibility for a herd of cows, I am married and have two children. I live in the same town as my family of origin. I have a lot of friends who mean the world to me. I am committed to the causes and dreams of others. The people who depend on me (and I on them) shape my everyday life. Before I met Tom, I had no idea what it was like to take care of a herd of dairy cows. After my visit with Tom, I found it helpful to compare my responsibility to the people who depend on me to the responsibility of milking cows. While my relatives and friends are not actually cows, they depend on me for their health and happiness nonetheless. The core practice of milk (your cows) is figuring out who depends on you and what it means to be committed to meeting their needs, while maintaining a sense of balance in your own life.

The night before I was scheduled to fly to Ohio, I was a bit nervous about visiting a farmer I had never met, whose closest neighbors were Amish people who had no phones or cars. What if my visit did not go well and I was stuck on a farm one hour from the nearest airport? Mary Cartledgehayes, a writer who lives in Ohio, had introduced me to Tom, but I did not know Mary all that well either. On the plane, however, I grew more and more certain that I was doing the right thing. One good way to grasp non-negotiable dependence, I figured, would be to spend some time with a guy who was responsible for hundreds of bulging udders every day, twice a day.

People who depend on you create demands that often appear to be non-negotiable. My dependents are children, a partner, aging parents, other family members, plants, pets, colleagues, and friends who expect a lot from me. I struggle to respond to and sometimes ignore these expectations. In the language of this particular practice, I feel that I must "milk" these dependents (i.e., attend to their needs) or they will suffer. Since most dependents do not present their needs in as clear a fashion as a cow and her udders, it has been important for me to spend time thinking about how to navigate these relationships and their attendant responsibilities. There is only so much of me to go around.

While I had a hunch that a dairy farmer might know something about time and dependence, I knew little about agriculture before I traveled to Ohio. In our hour-long drive from the Akron airport to Dalton, Tom's hometown, the signs paid homage to the old country. I saw Das Dutch Kitchen, Dalton Dairyette, and Handmade Baskets signs that appeared to have been untouched over the past forty years. As we neared the farm, Tom and I talked about his fifteen-year-old pot-bellied pig named Julia. He thought it was a pretty neat coincidence that his oldest animal and I had the same name. "She's in charge," he said, "but she's very docile. We give her doggy treats." Tom told me about his donkeys, ducks, and Jack Russell terrier. As he spoke, he stretched all of his vowels, making his voice sound like an accordion.

As we turned onto Tom's road and his 1200 acres, he told me about his family. His sisters Laura and Susan, one divorced and the other widowed, were near neighbors. They came over almost daily to help out at the farm, and both also had the responsibility of their families. His parents were in their late seventies and wintered in Florida. Tom lived in his grandparents' house, across the driveway from his mom and dad. His employees, past and present, were mostly helpful but had their own problems that kept them from being completely reliable. Despite all the helpers, the responsibility was squarely with Tom to manage the farm, to know when to lock in on the price of grain, and to order all of the supplies. When a piece of equipment did not work, he was the one to fix it.

Tom's house was a bachelor pad in the middle of a cornfield with only a collection of barns to keep it company. "I tried to clean up before you got here," he said as we walked in the house. He had a housekeeper, but she fell and broke her hip three years before. Tom lived primarily in the kitchen area of his house with a table full of reading material, a sink full of dishes, and a minimally stocked refrigerator. His desktop computer opened to the John Deere website; a John Deere Tiffany-style lamp and a fish tank stood nearby. An abundance of cow mugs populated the kitchen cupboard and counter. Time was relative in this landscape. It was 10:40 on one clock and 6:10 on the other. The computer said December 31, 1600. Calendars from the past five years were nailed one on top of the other beside the sink.

Across the gravel road from his house, Tom's "petting zoo" featured a variety of animals that depended on him for their care and feeding. A chicken-wire fence corralled an ornamental duck, two emus, and a peacock. The zoo's landscaping included a pond, some elephant ear plants, and pink impatiens. "I think the ducks are neat. I really enjoy that colorful duck," Tom said as he pointed in the direction of one. "There is always someone who is worthy of my attention." Tom mentioned the three donkeys grazing in another pasture and said, "I enjoy the heck out of my little donkeys."

Tom had work to do, so he helped me into his 20,000-pound John Deere chopper. It was October and yellow trees lined the road as we made our way to one of his cornfields. My seat was not fully bolted down, so I braced myself with one foot against the bottom of the windshield for a couple of hours as he harvested corn, six rows at a time. Tom's eyes constantly tracked the topography for ditches and stray cobs of corn. The corn bowed down before the big machine as it was sucked into the chopper and processed into grain. With fields in every direction, Tom talked about the risks he faced as a farmer. Once when a fire started in one of his silos, the firefighters who showed up wouldn't go inside. (Three firefighters had died in a similar fire a few years before.) Tom took one of their hoses, climbed in, and put out the fire. "I do risky things," he said. "But I try not to do stupid things."

"Hobby farmers" were common to the area. "Seeking nirvana is darn elusive," Tom said as he pondered the lives of his neighbors. "Every farmer has his or her own story." But he thought the hobby farmers could not deal with the common frustrations of farming. He pointed a couple of hills over to a farmer "who felt he was always right." The hobbyist never sought advice from the more experienced farmers like Tom who could have helped him through difficulties before they turned into disasters. When the farmer ran out of money to feed his cows, Tom filled the man's silo. Next, Tom pointed to a farm where they grew marijuana and said the Amish farmers nearby had busted them.

Farming is expensive. Vitamins, antibiotics, and protein supplements for the cows cost Tom dearly. Soil has to be prepped at just the right time for crops like corn and soybeans to grow properly. The work of proper cultivation and harvesting takes careful timing and hard labor. Tom said farmers can get lazy and wait too long to put in the crops. "People can make stupid decisions," he said. Weather determines the success or failure of a harvest, and Mother Nature can wreck the best-laid plans with drought or too much rain.

We rode in the chopper to Tom's house as dusk turned the landscape a warm orange glow. Just as we finished dinner, his dad opened the door asking when Tom would begin milking the cows. Bulging udders only wait so long. They don't tolerate sick or mental health days. Twice a day, Tom goes out to the pasture and leads the herd into the barn. Once inside, the cows settle into the twelve elevated stalls on either side of the barn. An aisle runs between the two rows of stalls; that's where Tom works. He wipes off bulging teats with a rag, sprays them with an antiseptic, makes one or two teats squirt, and then attaches the suction.

Our eyes were at belly level to the cows. While twelve cows were being milked, the other hundred-plus waited in the back of the barn. Many of them were not happy about going into a stall and put up a fight as Tom tried to coax them inside. The most recalcitrant ones hung at the back. They kicked and flinched, making it perilous for Tom as he wrestled them into place. I figured since I had breastfed my children, milking a cow would be easy. Tom said to give it a try. I looked at the long row of udders and chose the one with the biggest bulge. I wrapped my fingers around one of the teats and yanked as I had seen Tom doing. The cow stomped her foot in distress and no milk came out. It took an embarrassingly long time to get even a little squirt out, so I got out of the way and watched Tom from then on.

Tom explained that a milking session took about three hours from start to finish and said that most people with herds the size of his own hired people to milk their cows. They hired Mexican laborers or other people who would work for lower wages. It's labor-intensive work milking cows twice a day. Still, from Tom's point of view, if you didn't milk the cows yourself, how could you possibly get to know them? Yes, it's grueling. Yes, you were tied to the farm. But isn't that what you signed up for, Tom wondered?

As we talked (over the loud chugging of the milkers), I realized how removed Tom felt from other people, at times, even from his family and other farmers. He was almost always hard at work and mainly among animals. There was nothing lonelier, he said, than being with a group of people who were supposed to be like-minded, such as other farmers, and discovering you had little in common. Though neighbors, government officials, and family enjoyed being around Tom, his responsibilities required that he spend a lot of time alone.

I was exhausted and finally said good-night around nine that night. Tom still had another hour of work. As I walked outside the barn to Tom's house, I greeted Tom's five-year-old niece, who was making mud pies while her mom visited next door with her parents. I entered Tom's house by way of the kitchen, passed the computer and the fish tank, and went up a dark stairwell to an even darker guest room. It had still been light outside when we left to tend the cows. Sparky the dog was asleep on the guest bed. I pushed him off and settled under the covers. The chugging of the milk machines was the last sound I heard before falling into a deep sleep.

Since milking cows took up six or seven hours of every day, Tom had little time or energy for much else beyond farm chores. "A lot of the bad things stay out of my scope," he said. His time with the cows seemed to make him sensitive to the beauty of life all around him. Each phase of the moon, the fall colors, and the land filled him with wonder. In the midst of his responsibilities, he remained present to the beauty of his family farm.

Even though Tom's life has been taken up with cows that must be milked, corn that has to be harvested, and family members who need help, he remains open to spontaneity. Occasionally, Tom finds time to leave the farm, if only for a day or two. Once, he drove to Toronto to see the Broadway musical *Hair Spray* and a Canadian farm exhibition and was home within eighteen hours to milk the cows. He drove to Florida and back in a couple of days. Even though he drove straight through, he was mindful enough to be able to recommend places along the way for friends back home to see. "You have to make life special for yourself," he said.

On the morning of my departure, I could hear Tom's alarm clock in his bedroom downstairs. He was already gone to be with the cows and work on the rest of the farm, but his snooze alarm was wailing as if a real elephant were in the house. Tom had laid out an article about health and wellness for me to read over breakfast. He had also cut out a piece about creative writing by a local columnist. After sleeping so well, I was ecstatic to be surrounded by my new friends, the cows, donkeys, and the residents of the petting zoo. Best of all, I would return home grateful to have met Tom, a man who brought new perspective in my search for good busy.

On our way to the airport, Tom pointed out the Amish farms that bordered his family's property. In contrast to Tom's machinery, industrial-sized barns, and expansive fields of crops, the Amish farms represented an alternative, one that emphasized simplicity and self-sustainability. One farmer was working his field, but instead of a tractor, a horse was pulling his plow. Nearby, a woman was out in her yard hanging clothes on the line. Amish people in horse-drawn buggies joined us on the road. While having Amish neighbors was quaint, there had been occasional difficulties between the Amish and the rest of the farmers. "They come by our house to use our phone because they don't have their own. They are a real pain in the neck," Tom's dad said. But unlike the hobby farmers, the Amish earned their keep from the land.

As we approached the Akron airport, I asked Tom what the farm and he might become in the future. He said he hoped to build a milking barn twice the size of the one he had for a larger herd of cows. After the barn was built, he would measure his success by how clean and content the cows were. Happy cows and occasional road trips to places like Florida and Canada—that was enough. For Tom, the search for good busy meant reckoning with his own responsibility for the care of others without losing his sense of wonder for the life all around him.

10 **Hunt**

Discover the source of your busyness.

Sandy Dang sat up in bed at three A.M., unable to quell persistent fears that her non-profit organization had not raised enough money. In the stillness of her one-bedroom apartment in Washington, DC, she made a frantic scan of all she had to do in the next couple of days. There was a foundation report, a staff person with post-traumatic stress disorder, payroll, and the 2.5 million dollar capital campaign.

In the midst of her anxiety, an image appeared to Sandy, almost like a prayer, an image of her father from their days in Vietnam during the war. She remembered her father heading out into the dark each night to search for food for his family. A carpenter and mechanic by day, her father would leave their Hanoi home in the middle of the night to catch frogs for his family to eat. Wearing a self-fashioned construction hat with a battery-operated light, he went out to the swamps of Hanoi to hunt frogs with a long stick. His efforts could have cost him his life.

While Sandy has spent most of her life in the United States in relative safety, these memories of the war and her father's nightly search for nourishment for his family have shaped the person she is today. With degrees from Duke University and Catholic University of America, Sandy could have chosen stable employment with the promise of financial reward. Instead, she decided to become a social entrepreneur and launch an organization that helps Asian youth who face some of the same challenges she faced as an immigrant to the United States.

Sandy is the founder and president of Asian American LEAD (AALEAD), an organization in Washington, DC that provides social and educational services for Asian American youth and their families. Petite and impeccably dressed, with shoulder-length dark hair, Sandy has eyes that convey instant warmth as well as an urgency that limits rambling conversation. Because she came to this country as an older child, she continues to speak with an accent, which reminds me of her role as a broker between two worlds. Sandy and I met because she hired me as a time management coach.

After the coaching sessions came to an end, I asked if I could interview her about how her perspectives on busyness had been influenced by her life story. While I was disarmed by the matter-of-fact way she described the difficulties she had faced as a younger person, I knew such experiences allowed her to empathize with the young people involved in AALEAD.

As Sandy told me about her family's miraculous story of surviving the war and moving to the United States, her busyness began to make sense. Her tireless work on behalf of others came straight from her father's desperate efforts to save his family. Sandy's father's practice of hunting frogs during the war inspired Sandy's drive to do everything she can for people in need. Her commitment to other people shapes the way she organizes her daily life. When Sandy realized that her middle-of-the-night anxiety was related to her father's nights in the swamp, there was both peace and discomfort in her epiphany. Her busyness was like her father's, and it was also laced with a compulsion. Her overwhelming concern for others and her inability to sleep had roots in a father who was driven to take care of others. Sandy was her father's daughter, even though her swamp was our nation's capital. Instead of hunting food with a long stick, Sandy created educational opportunities to encourage Asian-American youth to fulfill their potential.

Listening to Sandy prompted me to think more deeply about how the busyness of my own parents, relatives, and friends may have influenced the choices I make every day. The way she planned and acted on what mattered to her was influenced by her upbringing, and especially by her father. I called Sandy's practice "hunt" in honor of her father, who risked his life to find nourishment for his family. In Sandy's own life, hunt has become a metaphor for seeking to understand the roots of her identity in work and the way she relates to the world.

I began to see a practice for all of us as I talked with Sandy. Whether you admit it or not, your relationship with busyness has probably been shaped by your parents, grandparents, or someone else from your childhood. Remember the important people from your childhood and what daily habits they kept. Most likely, you mimic someone you grew up with and observed, and whose habits you later embodied. Or perhaps your relationship with busyness is enacted in direct opposition to family members who approached or denied daily commitments in a manner that you found irritating as a child. Hunting for the source of our busyness allows us to take a look at our own patterns of activity with fresh eyes. Of the qualities you adopted in relation to the important people in your life, which ones serve your good busy now? Which do you want to keep, and which ones will you try to change?

The image of her parents' efforts fuels Sandy's activity. It is a constant reminder that, although her days are long and she is tired, her work is not as hard as trying to keep a family alive in the middle of a war. "We were so poor," she says, "and still, my parents found ways to make it good. Imagine if you had kids, and people were dying all around you. It was a very harsh reality, but I still have good memories of my childhood."

Sandy's family escaped Vietnam in 1977, when she was nine, and traveled to China to work on a sugar cane plantation. Two years later, they began a journey from China to British Hong Kong, living in six different refugee camps in three years. Sandy says, "We lived in a warehouse with rows of bunk beds housing two or three hundred people. My mom was pregnant. My dad had an accident where he broke his leg." Since neither parent could work, Sandy got a job in a factory that made waffle irons so the family could buy food.

Meanwhile, Sandy's grandmother was sponsored by a member of the Mormon Church and emigrated to the United States. In 1981, Sandy's grandmother began to arrange for the rest of the family to join her. She found another Mormon to sponsor Sandy and her family, and they made the trip from Hong Kong to Utah. At thirteen, Sandy started school in Salt Lake City, where there were no bilingual programs. Freed from work in fields and factories, she began the struggle to learn a new language and become acquainted with yet another culture.

Not long after their arrival, Sandy's family grew uncomfortable with the rules of the Mormon Church. "I came all the way to the United States, and you tell me not to drink, not to smoke?" her father complained. So the family moved to Brooklyn, New York and into an apartment that cost $200 a month. Her dad got a job, her mom went to work sewing in a factory, and Sandy became a straight "A" student.

Sandy says it is often hard for an immigrant child to find a place to belong. "When you are an immigrant or a refugee, there is a tremendous sense of loss—loss of a country, loss of a way of life and extended family. A lot of people don't understand. They say, 'Oh, you're so lucky you live in the United States.'" But Sandy wasn't always lucky. While living in Brooklyn, she would come home and lock her door because she was so frightened in her dangerous neighborhood. "Part of my longing has been for community and connection," she explains. AALEAD, the organization Sandy founded, gives at least some Asian-American kids a place to belong.

AALEAD's mission is to promote the well-being of Asian-American youth through education, leadership, and community building. By capturing millions of dollars from federal and private sources, the agency is able to provide mentoring and afterschool programs to thousands of underserved Asian-American young people in the Washington, DC metropolitan area. Its educational enrichment and youth development programs range from reading and writing to college prep and leadership development.

Though we could not have grown up in two more different circumstances, Sandy and I were both influenced by fathers who were devoted to their work. My father has been a radiologist at a big teaching hospital in North Carolina for most of my life. As a child I would stride down the hospital corridors beside my dad, proud that I could keep up with his long legs and fast clip. Never slowing his pace, he greeted everyone he passed in the hall. He was in his element at work, and I inhaled his confidence. Not all my memories of my father's dedication to work are happy ones. He was called to the hospital at all hours of the day and night, and his beeper would go off at the most inopportune moments—in the middle of a piano recital or on Christmas morning.

Reflecting on Sandy's three A.M. revelation, I can see how much I am like my dad. I walk fast everywhere I go and prefer days with an agenda. When Dad read x-rays in the darkest rooms of the hospital, he got into a state of flow. I have always loved working at my desk alone, even finding a certain ecstasy in multitasking. Dad has always been more comfortable wearing a white coat and attending to ill people than kicking back at a barbeque. I am more comfortable standing in front of a classroom of students than holding a beer and making small talk at a party. Now in his eighties, he continues to teach and practice medicine. Dad still shows up at work at six in the morning to instruct medical students and brief his colleagues. Most days, I get a thrill out of running to catch the city bus early in the morning in order to get to campus to teach or study. Dad loves his work and so do I. Like Sandy, the hunt for the source of my own good busyness begins and ends with my father.

Discovering the source of your busyness isn't always a pleasant revelation, but leveling blame or praise at a close relative will only slow down your search for good busy. For years, I harbored resentment toward my dad for his absence at home. These blaming tendencies only obscured the fact that, as I grew up, I was turning into a female version of my dad. When I began to own up to the fact that I too had a zeal for work, sometimes to the detriment of my nuclear family, I realized whatever blame I placed on him was a critique of myself, because my busyness is my choice. I had to learn how to make peace with the past. Sandy's story taught me to figure out whose busyness I had adopted and to accept responsibility for my daily choices and actions now. Just as I inherited my dad's long legs, I also inherited his zeal for a fast-paced life, and I depend on both for my sense of who I am. My interviews with Sandy played a significant role in helping me attain some peace about my father and about my own busyness.

Learning how to identify the source of our busyness

will further any search for good busy. Like any behavior we have that isn't helpful, identifying the source allows us to see why we behave the way we do—to bring unconscious behavior to light. Once we're aware of our unconscious behavior, we can choose to change it if it doesn't serve us any more, or continue with it if it does.

It is crucial to remember that the source of our busyness may not be the person we mimic in our everyday lives, but rather the one we rebel against. While Sandy and I resemble the busyness of our fathers, other people in this search for good busy have rebelled against their source. Kari's buffer practice was developed in response to a childhood that lacked any margin of predictability or control. Esther has learned how to navigate the Gungee in her life, not out of a desire to be like her family of origin in Oregon, but to demonstrate that patience and persistence can make possible a different outcome. Rebelling against the source of our busyness can be just as powerful a motivator as mimicking. Being aware of our past choices and deciding if they still work for us is an important step to crafting our own definition of good busy.

CHAPEL HILL PUBLIC LIBRARY

3 5064 00486 7847

FEB 2013

RETIRED

chapelhillpubliclibrary.org